The Ultimate Women's Guide to F'
Exercises and Workouts

# THE ULTIMATE WOMEN'S GUIDE TO FITNESS: FAT-BURNING EXERCISES AND WORKOUTS

The Ultimate Women's Guide to Fitness: Fat-Burning Exercises and Workouts

**Copyright © 2023 by Cleopatra Noble

All rights reserved. No part of this publication may be reproduced, distributed, or transmitted in any form or by any means, including photocopying, recording, or other electronic or mechanical methods, without the prior written permission of the publisher, except in the case of brief quotations embodied in critical reviews and certain other noncommercial uses permitted by copyright law.

This book is a work of general reference and does not provide personalized medical or fitness advice. The author and publisher are not responsible for any specific health or fitness outcomes that may result from reading this book. Readers are advised to consult with healthcare and fitness professionals before embarking on any exercise or diet program.

First Edition: 2023

The Ultimate Women's Guide to Fitness: Fat-Burning Exercises and Workouts

**Disclaimer**

This book, "The Ultimate Women's Guide to Fitness: Fat-Burning Exercises and Workouts," is intended for informational purposes only. The information contained within this book is not a substitute for professional medical, health, or fitness advice, diagnosis, or treatment. Before beginning any new exercise, program or making significant changes to your diet or lifestyle, it is crucial to consult with a qualified healthcare professional or fitness expert. Individual health and fitness needs vary, and what works for one person may not be suitable for another.

The author and publisher of this book have made reasonable efforts to provide accurate and up-to-date information. However, they do not warrant the accuracy, completeness, or fitness for a particular purpose of the information presented within these pages. The author and publisher do not assume any responsibility for any potential health or safety issues that may arise from the use of the exercises, techniques, or recommendations contained in this book.

Readers must take personal responsibility for their health and safety and should use their best judgment when following any exercise or dietary guidance provided in this book. It is recommended to consult a healthcare professional before making any significant changes to your fitness or dietary routines, especially if you have any pre-existing medical conditions or concerns.

The author and publisher disclaim any liability, loss, or risk directly or indirectly incurred as a consequence of applying any information presented in this book. By reading this book, you acknowledge and accept the terms of this disclaimer.

Remember: Safety should always be the top priority when engaging in physical activities

**and making changes to your health and fitness regimen.**

## About the Author

Cleopatra Noble is a renowned Counseling Psychologist and a trailblazing influencer in the realm of personal development. With a passion for helping individuals unlock their full potential, she has dedicated her career to empowering others to lead more fulfilling lives.

Cleopatra is the visionary behind "Timeout With Cleopatra," a highly acclaimed YouTube channel that she created to inspire, motivate, and enlighten individuals on their journey to self-improvement. Her channel has garnered a loyal following, thanks to her engaging and insightful content that offers practical advice and wisdom for personal growth.

With a background in Counseling Psychology, Cleopatra brings a wealth of knowledge and expertise to her work. Her empathetic and compassionate approach has touched the lives of countless viewers, guiding them through life's challenges and encouraging them to embrace positive change.

Cleopatra Noble's commitment to the well-being and personal development of others has earned her a reputation as a trusted mentor and motivator. Through her online platform and various speaking engagements, she continues to impact lives, helping individuals become the best versions of themselves.

Join Cleopatra on her transformative journey of self-discovery and empowerment, as she shares her wisdom and insights to inspire positive change in the lives of her audience.

Connect with Cleopatra Noble:

-Timeout With Cleopatra – www.youtube.com/@timeoutwithcleopatra

- Email: timeoutwithcleopatra@gmail.com

The Ultimate Women's Guide to Fitness: Fat-Burning Exercises and Workouts

## TABLE OF CONTENTS

Introduction ................................................................................8
Chapter 1: Women's Health and Fitness ...................................11
Chapter 2: Managing Your Diet .................................................17
Chapter 3: Fat-Losing Cardiovascular Exercises........................23
Chapter 4: Women's Strength Training ......................................29
Chapter 5: Adaptability and Equilibrium....................................35
Chapter 6: Creating a Customized Exercise Schedule................40
Chapter 7: Remaining secure and free from harm ....................46
Chapter 8: Fitness Psychology ...................................................51
Chapter 9: Long-Term Health and Lifestyle ..............................56
Chapter 10: Accepting Inner Strength and Moving Past the Physical .......................................................................................61
Conclusion: Your Path to a Happier, Healthier You ..................64

## Introduction

Welcome to "The Ultimate Women's Guide to Fitness: Fat-Burning Exercises and Workouts." This book is a comprehensive resource designed to empower women with the knowledge and tools they need to embark on a transformative journey toward better health and fitness.

In an age where health and wellness have taken center stage, the quest for a fit and vibrant lifestyle has never been more prevalent. Women, in particular, often find themselves juggling numerous responsibilities, from careers and family to personal pursuits. It's in this demanding landscape that we aim to provide a guiding light, helping you find the balance between your well-being and the myriad roles you play.

This book is more than a mere collection of exercise routines and diet plans; it's a holistic approach to fitness tailored to women's unique needs and goals. We understand that every woman's body is distinct, and their aspirations and challenges vary. Whether you're starting your fitness journey or looking to revitalize your existing routine, "The Ultimate Women's Guide to Fitness" will provide you with the insights and strategies to achieve your goals.

Throughout these pages, we'll delve into the essential principles of fitness, exploring the science behind fat-burning exercises, nutrition, and the psychology of motivation. You'll find expertly crafted workout routines that cater to different fitness levels, ensuring that everyone can find a path to success.

However, it's crucial to remember that fitness is not just about achieving a certain physique—it's about feeling strong, confident, and healthy in your own skin. This book is not about promoting unrealistic beauty standards; instead, it's a guide to help you build strength, endurance, and resilience, both physically and mentally. It's about celebrating progress, no matter how small, and embracing the journey towards a healthier you.

As you embark on this fitness adventure, we encourage you to approach it with patience and kindness towards yourself. Understand that transformation takes time, effort, and dedication. Be open to learning and adapting, and most importantly, listen to your body. Your path to fitness should be as unique as you are, and this guide will be your trusty companion along the way.

So, let's embark on this journey together—unleash your inner strength, boost your confidence, and take charge of your health. "The Ultimate Women's Guide to Fitness: Fat-Burning Exercises and Workouts" is your roadmap to a healthier, happier, and more energetic you. Let's get started!

The Ultimate Women's Guide to Fitness: Fat-Burning Exercises and Workouts

## Chapter 1: Women's Health and Fitness

With so many obligations, expectations, and daily demands in today's world, it can be very simple for a woman to neglect her physical well-being. Self-care is frequently neglected on the life treadmill. But in this chapter, we're going to teach you that prioritizing your health is a vital component of a well-rounded, satisfying existence, not merely a self-indulgent gesture. Let's explore the value of physical fitness for women, the advantages of consistent exercise, and the skill of goal-setting that works.

**Recognizing the Importance of Female Fitness**

There's more to women's fitness than just squeezing into their favorite pair of pants or looking nice in a swimsuit. It's about developing a strong, capable, and resilient body and mind. Our distinct physical and psychological requirements demand a deliberate and customized approach to exercise. This is the reason why:

1. **Health and Longevity**: Heart disease, diabetes, and some types of cancer can be avoided in large part by adopting a balanced diet and engaging in regular physical activity. Furthermore, leading an active life can help you live a longer, more fulfilling life.

2. **Mental Well-Being**: Exercise is an effective means of preserving mental health in addition to its physical advantages. It can improve cognitive performance and self-esteem while lowering stress, anxiety, and sadness.

3. **Empowerment:** Being physically fit promotes self-assurance, empowerment, and a feeling of achievement. Your job and relationships, as well as other aspects of your life, can benefit from setting and accomplishing fitness goals.

4. **Independence**: For women to stay independent as we age, we must continue to be strong and mobile. Engaging in regular exercise can support us in maintaining our independence far into old age.

5. **Hormonal Balance:** Since exercise helps control hormones, it's especially crucial for women's hormonal health. It can lessen the signs and symptoms of menopause and PMS.

**The Advantages of Frequent Exercise**

Let's now examine the many benefits that ladies might experience from regular exercise. These advantages go well beyond the material world:

1. **Weight Management:** One useful strategy for controlling weight is exercise. It facilitates the maintenance of a healthy weight by increasing metabolism, burning calories, and constructing lean muscle.

2. **Enhanced Energy Levels**: Engaging in regular physical activity makes you feel more energized and less fatigued, giving you the endurance to go about your everyday business and fully enjoy life.

3. **Better Sleep**: Physical activity can help you get the rest and renewal your body needs to perform at its best.

4. **Stress Reduction**: Exercise causes the body's natural stress relievers, endorphins, to

be released. You'll be able to handle the stressors of modern life better with this.

5. **Strengthened Immune System**: Physical activity boosts immunity, increasing resistance to diseases and infections.

6. **Improved Heart Health:** Exercise that involves the heart is essential for heart health. It lowers blood pressure and cholesterol, which lowers the risk of heart disease.

7. **Enhanced Cognitive performance**: Research has connected physical exercise to enhanced memory, cognitive performance, and general brain health. It enhances the brain naturally.

8. **Improving Mental Health:** Frequent exercise helps lessen the signs of anxiety and despair and encourage a happier mindset.

9. **Better Body Image**: You're likely to have a more positive body image and higher self-esteem as you get stronger and more self-assured via exercise.

10. **Social Connection**: Engaging in team sports or group exercise can foster meaningful social relationships and a feeling of community.

## Having Reasonable Objectives

The first step towards increased fitness is to create reasonable and doable objectives. Long-term success frequently requires a more gradual and sustained strategy, despite the temptation to try for quick, spectacular changes.

Realistic goal-setting entails:

1. **Setting Your Goals**: What do you hope to accomplish on your path to fitness? Clearly state your goals, whether they are to lose weight, tone your muscles, become more flexible, or increase your endurance.

2. **Specifying and Measuring Your Objectives:** General objectives such as "get in shape" are difficult to monitor. Instead, make clear, quantifiable goals like "run a 5K in under 30 minutes" or "lose 10 pounds in three months."

3. **Breaking Your Goals Down:** Split up your more ambitious objectives into more doable, smaller benchmarks. These little victories will help you stay inspired and on course.

4. **Creating a Reasonable Schedule**: Exercise self-compassion. Understand that significant changes require time. Anticipating too quickly might lead to irritation, so set a reasonable deadline.

5. **Tracking Your success:** To keep track of your success, use digital tools or keep a fitness notebook. You can celebrate your accomplishments and maintain accountability by doing this.

6. **Modifying Your Objectives as Needed**: Life is full of surprises, so you may need to modify your objectives as you go. Be pliable and adaptive in how you conduct yourself.

Recall that your journey to fitness is unique. The most crucial element is your dedication to enhancing your wellbeing. You have the ability to change your life, regardless of where you are in your fitness journey. We'll provide you the resources, information, and motivation you need to bring that transition to life in the ensuing chapters, towards a more powerful, content, and healthy version of yourself!

## Chapter 2: Managing Your Diet

This chapter will examine the vital role that nutrition plays in women's fitness, with an emphasis on understanding macronutrients and micronutrients, feeding your body for success, and mastering the art of eating for energy and well-being.

**Sustaining Your Body for Achievement**

Nutrition is the process of providing your body with fuel, not only the food you eat. Your body needs the optimum nutrients to function at its peak, much like an automobile needs the right kind of fuel to run well. So let's dissect how to fuel your body for success:

1. Balanced Diet: A balanced diet is made up of a range of items from several food categories. Make sure that a variety of fruits,

vegetables, whole grains, lean meats, and healthy fats are included in your meals.

2. Portion Control: To prevent overindulging, be mindful of portion proportions. To keep portion control, use gadgets like food scales and measuring cups.

3. Frequent Meals: Eating throughout the day at regular intervals keeps energy levels consistent and discourages overindulging.

4. Hydration: It's important to maintain proper hydration. Digestion, circulation, and temperature control all require water. Drink 8 or more glasses of water a day

5. Mindful Eating: Mindful eating involves paying attention to your body's signals of hunger and fullness, enjoying your food, and putting away outside distractions.

6. Meal and Snack Planning: Make your meal and snack plans in advance. This lessens the possibility of making snap decisions that aren't as healthful.

**Having a knowledge of macro- and micronutrients**

You must comprehend the macro- and micronutrient building blocks of nutrition in order to make wise dietary choices.

1. Nutrients in macro:

Choose complex carbs for long-lasting energy, such as those found in fruits, vegetables, and whole grains.

Proteins: Building and repairing muscle requires proteins. Incorporate into your diet lean foods such as fish, chicken, beans, and tofu.

Fats: Good fats aid in the generation of hormones among other physiological processes. Avocados, almonds, seeds, and olive oil are examples of sources.

2. Tiny nutrition:

Vitamins: These natural substances are essential for many body functions. Since vitamins can be found in a variety of foods, eating a varied diet is essential to get all the vitamins you need.

Minerals: For the health of bones, muscles, and oxygen transport, minerals like calcium, magnesium, and iron are essential. Lean meats, dairy, and leafy greens are excellent sources.

## Eating for Health and Vitality

Energy and well-being should come first in your food choices. Here are some tips for optimizing your mealtimes:

1. Go for Whole Foods: Whole foods are high in fiber and vital nutrients, like fresh produce, whole grains, and unprocessed meats.

2. Reduce your intake of processed foods: These foods frequently have too much salt, sugar, and bad fats.

3. Lean Protein: Make sure your diet includes lean protein sources such beans, fish, chicken, and low-fat dairy.

4. Fiber: Foods high in fiber, such as legumes and whole grains, facilitate better digestion, increase feelings of fullness, and help control blood sugar levels.

5. Healthy Fats: Include foods high in fat in your diet, such as olive oil, avocados, almonds, and seeds. The heart and brain are supported by these lipids.

6. Balanced Macronutrients: To supply you the energy you need for everyday activities and exercise, your meals should have a healthy proportion of fats, proteins, and carbohydrates.

7. Vitamins and Minerals: Make sure you eat a variety of foods to acquire the vitamins and minerals you need. In the event that you have particular dietary issues, think about speaking with a medical professional or nutritionist.

8. Hydration: To be hydrated, consistently consume water. Drinking enough water promotes good digestion, general health, and athletic performance.

As you set out on your fitness path, keep in mind that proper nutrition is essential to your success. It's about fueling your body, maintaining your energy, and improving your general health—not about denying yourself or adhering to rigid diets. We'll provide you advice in the upcoming chapters on workouts and regimens that go well with your dietary decisions and help you become a stronger, healthier, and more energetic version of yourself.

When you give your body the right fuel, it will reward you with the vitality and energy you need to reach your fitness objectives.

## Chapter 3: Fat-Losing Cardiovascular Exercises

Exercises that involve cardiovascular activity, sometimes abbreviated as "cardio," are an effective weapon in your fitness toolbox, especially if losing extra body fat is your objective. This chapter will cover the benefits of cardio as a fat-burning ally, women-specific cardio workouts that are beneficial, and the art of designing a personalized cardio program.

**Cardiovascular Power: An Ally for Burning Fat**

Cardio exercises are well known for their ability to burn fat. They speed up your heart rate, burn more calories, and contribute to the energy deficit required for weight loss. The following explains why cardio is such a useful tool for your fitness quest:

1. Caloric Expenditure: Cardio exercises burn calories, which makes them a useful method of establishing a calorie deficit—a necessary condition for fat loss.

2. Heart Health: Engaging in cardiovascular activity lowers the risk of heart disease by strengthening the heart and enhancing circulation.

3. Versatility: Cardio exercises may be done in a variety of ways, so you can pick exercises that you enjoy doing, like swimming, dancing, or cycling.

4. Increased Endurance: Consistent cardiac exercise increases endurance, which lessens the strain of everyday tasks.

5. Mental Health Benefits: Exercise is proven to lower stress and elevate mood, fostering a feeling of wellbeing.

6. Fat Mobilization: By encouraging the body to burn fat that has been stored as fuel, cardio exercises can help you lose weight while maintaining lean muscle mass.

Cardio Exercises That Work for Women

There are certain aerobic exercises that are better than others at helping you lose weight.

There are many different types of cardio exercises available to women, so it's critical to select activities that are both fun and beneficial. The following aerobic activities are exclusive to women:

1. Running: Running is a great way to increase your heart rate and burn calories, whether you choose to jog slowly or sprint. It offers versatility since it may be done on a treadmill or outside.

2. Cycling: Bicycling is a gentle on the joints, low-impact workout activity. You can ride a bike outside or utilize a stationary bike at home or in the gym.

3. Swimming: This low-impact exercise works the entire body and is gentle on the joints. If you want to tone your entire body, this is a great option.

4. Jump Rope: This easy-to-learn but efficient activity provides a quick, intense cardio workout virtually anyplace.

5. Dancing: You can make cardio seem like a fun and engaging activity by incorporating

dancing, hip-hop, or Zumba, which will help you stick with it.

6. High-Intensity Interval Training (HIIT): HIIT consists of quick bursts of high-intensity exercise interspersed with short rest intervals. It's ideal for busy women because it's effective and saves time.

7. Group Classes: A lot of gyms feature group exercises like circuit training, step aerobics, and spinning, which may be energizing and socializing.


Establishing a Cardio Workout

Your cardiac exercise program should be long-lasting and efficient. Here's how to create a cardio schedule that works for your schedule and helps you reach your fitness objectives:


1. Establish Specific Goals: Specify your levels of fitness. Do you want to increase your endurance, reduce weight, or just reap the psychological rewards of cardio?

2. Select Pleasurable Activities: Opt for cardiovascular workouts that you actually

enjoy. Long-term consistency with your routine will be facilitated by this.

3. Start Slow: As your fitness level rises, progressively increase the lengths and intensities of your workouts if you're new to them.

4. Mix It Up: To avoid boredom and target various muscle groups, including a range of aerobic activities.

5. Make a Schedule: Choose a time to perform your aerobic exercises. Because scheduling your sessions around your everyday schedule can help you stay consistent, do so.

6. Monitor Your Progress: To stay accountable and motivated, track your cardio sessions using a workout notebook or fitness applications.

7. Listen to Your Body: Observe how your cardio exercise makes you feel. As necessary, modify your plan to avoid overtraining and injuries.

Cardio is a crucial part of any fitness journey, particularly if you want to lose body fat. You can get in shape and lose weight by learning the advantages of cardiovascular exercise, selecting routines that work for you, and creating a customized cardio program.

## Chapter 4: Women's Strength Training

Strength training is a crucial but sometimes misunderstood aspect of women's fitness. This chapter will cover the benefits of toning and growing lean muscle as well as the misconceptions and realities surrounding strength training. It will also offer guidance on creating a customized strength training program.

**The Strength Training Myths and Truths**

There are several fallacies around strength training for women that need to be debunked. Let we differentiate between reality and imagination:

Myth 1: Women Get Bulky from Strength Training.

Truth: Gaining too much muscle mass is not the result of strength training alone. It supports women's efforts to develop toned, sculpted bodies and lean muscle.

**Myth 2: Strength training puts joints at risk.**

Truth: Strength training can lower the chance of injury and increase joint stability when done correctly. Technique and form are crucial.

**Myth 3: Only the Young Should Engage in Strength Training.**

Truth: Women of all ages benefit from strength training. As women age, it's especially crucial for preserving bone density.

**Myth 4: Big Weights Are Needed for Strength Training.**

Truth: Bodyweight exercises and light to moderate weights are two effective resistance levels for strength training.

**Myth 5: You Get Slower With Strength Training.**

The truth is that strength training can improve functional fitness, which will facilitate daily tasks and boost sports performance.

## Gaining Tone and Lean Muscle

Strength training aims to achieve a well-defined, toned physique, raise metabolic rate, and grow lean muscle rather than bulk up. How it helps is as follows:

1. Increased Metabolism: Maintaining lean muscle takes more energy, which raises your resting metabolic rate and aids in weight management.

2. Better Muscle Definition: Strength training tones and sculpts your muscles, making your physique look toned and solid.

3. Increased Strength: Having stronger muscles facilitates daily tasks and improves your physical capabilities.

4. Bone Health: As women age, strength exercise lowers their risk of osteoporosis by increasing bone density.

5. Better Posture: By fortifying the back and core muscles, strength training aids in the correction of posture problems.

## Creating a Program for Strength Training

Creating a strength training regimen is necessary to get the best possible outcomes. To make a plan that works for you, follow these steps:

1. Establish Your Objectives: Establish the goals you have for your strength training. Is it more strength, more muscular tone, or both?

2. Exercise Selection: Go for a range of exercises that focus on various muscle groups. Incorporate both isolation exercises (focusing on a single muscle area) and complex motions (working many muscle groups).

3. Establish Your Frequency: Try to do two or three strength training sessions a week at the very least. For optimal recuperation, give yourself 48 hours between exercises that focus on the same muscle area.

4. Determine Repetitions and Sets: For every exercise, determine how many repetitions (reps) and sets are required. Choose higher weights and fewer repetitions (4-6) to increase your strength and muscle mass. Use

moderate weights and try for higher reps (10–15) when toning.

5. Preserve Correct Form: Safety and efficacy depend on proper form. Consult a fitness expert for advice or make use of educational materials.

6. Progression: To keep your muscles challenged as you gain strength, progressively increase the weight or resistance.

7. Warm-Up and Cool-Down: To prepare your muscles and joints, always warm up before weight training. Cool down to increase flexibility and lessen soreness in your muscles.

8. Monitor Your Development: Maintain a log of your workouts, weights, and advancement. This enables you to celebrate your successes and modify your program.

9. Schedule Rest Days: Plan rest days between strength training sessions to give your muscles time to heal.

Strength training is a great complement to any exercise regimen, with many advantages that go beyond appearance. It's an investment in your general wellbeing, vitality, and health. We'll go into detail about particular strength training exercises, workout plans, and professional advice in the chapters that follow to help you reach your fitness objectives. This chapter lays the groundwork for your journey to a more toned, stronger, and healthier version of yourself, regardless of your level of experience with lifting.

Overcoming obstacles that you previously believed were insurmountable is the source of strength.

## Chapter 5: Adaptability and Equilibrium

Flexibility and balance are two facets of women's fitness that are frequently disregarded in the pursuit of total wellness and fitness. This chapter will discuss the importance of flexibility for women's fitness, the ways that yoga and Pilates can improve balance, and how to easily combine both flexibility and balance into your exercise regimen.

### The Significance of Flexibility in Women's Exercise

The foundational aspect of women's fitness that is sometimes overlooked is flexibility. It's essential to your general health to be able to move your joints and muscles through their entire range of motion. This is why adaptability is important:

1. Injury Prevention: Joints and muscles that are flexible are less likely to get injured. Sprains, strains, and overuse injuries are less common in people with a wide range of motion.

2. Improved Posture: Maintaining proper posture lowers the chance of musculoskeletal issues by promoting flexibility.

3. Stress Reduction: Practicing stretches and flexibility exercises helps reduce stress, promote physical relaxation, and enhance mental health.

4. Better Performance: Enhanced sports performance and everyday mobility can result from increased flexibility.

5. Pain Relief: Stretching helps lessen chronic pain and ease tense muscles.

## Pilates, Yoga, and Other Exercises that Promote Balance

Popular exercises like yoga and Pilates improve flexibility while also fostering strength, balance, and general wellbeing. Let's examine these practices' advantages:

1. Yoga: Yoga is a holistic discipline that incorporates meditation, breathing techniques (pranayama), and physical postures (asanas). It's well known to enhance balance, flexibility, and stress reduction. Different styles of yoga,

including Hatha, Vinyasa, and Bikram, offer varying degrees of focus and intensity.

2. Pilates: Pilates is a set of exercises meant to improve balance, flexibility, and core strength. It emphasizes precise, controlled motions to strengthen the core, lower back, hips, and buttocks—the body's powerhouse.

3. Tai Chi: Tai Chi is a Chinese martial technique that incorporates deep breathing with fluid, languid motions. It enhances mental clarity, balance, and coordination.

4. Balance Training: Stability, coordination, and posture are all enhanced by balance exercises like standing on one leg or utilizing balance boards.

## Including Balance and Flexibility in Your Daily Routine

Exercising balance and flexibility doesn't have to be difficult or time-consuming. Here's how to include them in an easy way:

1. Warm-Up and Cool-Down: Stretching should be done both before and after an exercise session to warm up your muscles

and to help them relax. This lowers the chance of damage and increases flexibility.

2. Committed Sessions: Arrange regular Tai Chi, Pilates, or yoga classes. These exercises provide a special fusion of stress relief, balance, and flexibility.

3. Workouts at Home: You can perform a lot of stretches and balance drills at home. Think about including them in your regular regimen, even if it's just a little stretch in the morning or a balancing drill before bed.

4. Balance Challenges: Work on your balance while performing regular tasks, such as standing in line or brushing your teeth with one leg. Over time, these modest efforts can have a significant impact.

5. Set Objectives: Just like with strength or cardio training, set objectives for balance and flexibility. Evaluate your development and acknowledge your successes.

Not only are flexibility and balance vital for maintaining your physical health and preventing injuries, but they also help you reach your fitness goals in general. You may improve your physical skills and foster mental peace by adding activities that increase

The Ultimate Women's Guide to Fitness: Fat-Burning
Exercises and Workouts

flexibility, such as yoga and Pilates, to your routine. We'll go into more detail on particular exercises and routines in the upcoming chapters to help you become more flexible and balanced and ultimately become a more resilient, nimble, and harmonious version of yourself.

*A balanced, flexible life is essential for overall well-being and grace.*

## Chapter 6: Creating a Customized Exercise Schedule

Your quest for greater fitness is an individual and distinctive undertaking. We will get into the art of creating a customized exercise regimen in this chapter. Setting your fitness objectives, creating your weekly workout routine, and staying motivated while breaking through plateaus are all part of this strategy.

**Choosing Your Fitness Objectives**

Every effective fitness journey starts with clearly stated objectives. In addition to offering direction, setting attainable goals also acts as a source of inspiration. Here's how to properly set your fitness objectives:

1. Specificity: Clearly state your objectives. Choose precise objectives like "losing 15 pounds in four months" or "completing a 5K run in under 30 minutes" in place of an ambiguous one like "getting in shape."

2. Measurability: Ensure that your objectives can be measured. This enables you to monitor advancement and recognize successes. You

can track improvements in strength, endurance, or weight loss.

3. Realism: Your objectives ought to be reachable. Although having ambition is admirable, having unattainable goals can cause disappointment and dissatisfaction. Think about how fit you are right now and how much time you can actually dedicate to your workouts.

4. Time Frame: Set a deadline for achieving your objectives. A deadline instills drive and a feeling of urgency. It supports your commitment and helps you monitor your progress.

5. Flexibility: Keep an open mind and be willing to modify your plans as needed. Because life is dynamic, you may need to make modifications along the road as you pursue health.

6. Write Them Down: Clearly state your objectives. It gives them a more authentic feel and offers a point of reference for future reviews and assessments.

## Creating Your Weekly Workout Program

After you've determined your fitness objectives, it's time to design a regimented exercise program to help you reach those goals. When creating your plan, take the following into account:

1. Balance: Combine activities for flexibility, strength training, cardiovascular fitness, and balance. This comprehensive strategy improves general fitness.

2. Frequency: Work out how frequently you can actually commit to working out. The majority of specialists advise exercising three to five days a week at the very least.

3. Length: Establish the length of each training session. Given your lifestyle, your schedule ought to be sustainable and manageable.

4. Rest Days: Schedule rest days to give your body a chance to heal and to avoid overtraining. In order to restore muscles and avoid burnout, rest is crucial.

5. Variety: Add a range of activities and exercises to your regimen to keep it fresh. In

addition to keeping things interesting, variety works various muscle areas.

6. Adaptation: Be ready to modify your plan in light of your development and evolving situation. This adaptability guarantees that you can keep working toward your objectives even in the face of unforeseen circumstances.

## Remaining Inspired and Breaking Through Obstacles

One of the common challenges on the path to better fitness is staying motivated. Here's how you break through blocks and maintain inspiration:

1. Monitor Your Progress: Document your workout accomplishments in a journal. Acknowledge minor accomplishments along the journey to serve as a reminder of your progress.

2. Establish Rewards: Provide incentives when attaining specified goals. This might be a new training attire, a treat, or any other motivating thing.

3. Find a Workout Partner: Enrolling in group classes or working out with a friend might help with accountability and inspiration.

4. Vary It Up: When your body becomes accustomed to a routine, plateaus may appear. To challenge your body in fresh ways, vary your routines and attempt new activities.

5. Mentality: Retain an optimistic outlook. Visualize your success and have faith in your capacity to reach your objectives.

6. Seek Professional Advice: If you find it difficult to maintain motivation or reach a plateau, you might want to speak with a coach or fitness expert. Their knowledge might offer fresh viewpoints and approaches.

Creating a customized exercise program is a dynamic process. It changes as you advance and adapt to new situations. Setting specific objectives, creating a well-rounded weekly workout plan, and maintaining motivation to push through plateaus can help you make sure your fitness journey is rewarding, long-lasting, and customized to your own requirements.

The Ultimate Women's Guide to Fitness: Fat-Burning
Exercises and Workouts

We'll give you personalized routines, professional advice, and tactics in the upcoming chapters to help you reach your fitness objectives. You will soon be stronger, healthier, and more confident with your customized exercise program in place.

*Your objectives serve as your life's road maps, guiding you and illuminating the possibilities.*

## Chapter 7: Remaining secure and free from harm

Safety is the first thing you should think about while you work for your fitness objectives. This chapter will cover typical exercise-related injuries, prevention techniques, the value of using proper form during exercises, and when to seek medical advice to ensure your safety and wellbeing.

**The Significance of Correct Form**

The cornerstone of safe and efficient exercise is proper form. It guarantees that you're working the appropriate muscle groups, lowering your chance of injury, and getting the most out of every workout. This is the reason it's vital:

1. Injury Prevention: Using proper form reduces the chance of sprains, strains, and other ailments associated with exercise.

2. Targeted Muscle Engagement: Using proper form guarantees that you are engaging the targeted muscle groups, which will help

you reach your fitness objectives more successfully.

3. Better Results: You'll experience improvements in your strength, endurance, and general performance when you complete exercises with proper form.

4. Posture and Alignment: You may enhance your posture and general body alignment by practicing proper technique during your workouts.

5. Confidence: Maintaining your exercise regimen is more likely when you are motivated and feel that you are employing correct form.

## Typical Exercise-Related Injuries and How to Avoid Them

While accidents resulting from exercise are not impossible, many are avoidable. The following list of typical injuries and preventative measures:

1. Strains and Sprains: Overexertion, improper form, and lack of warm-up can lead to muscle strains and ligament sprains. To prevent these, warm up, use proper form, and avoid lifting excessive weights.

2. Tendinitis: This inflammation of the tendons is brought on by overuse and repetitive motions. Avoid it by mixing up your workouts, exercising with the right form, and giving yourself enough time to recover.

3. Stress Fractures: Running and other high-impact exercises can cause stress fractures. Use proper footwear, mix up your exercise routine, and make sure you're getting enough calcium into your diet to avoid them.

4. Back discomfort: Inadequate form during physical activities, particularly those involving the back, can give rise to back discomfort. To avoid back problems, keep your posture straight, lift objects with care, and develop your core.

5. Joint Problems: Over time, joint problems may arise from high-impact activities. Vary your exercise regimen to lessen the impact on your joints and make sure your footwear is appropriate for the activities you perform to lower the risk.

6. Overtraining: Excessive training can result in fatigue, poor performance, and a higher chance of injury. Schedule rest days and pay

attention to your body's cues to avoid overtraining.

**When to Look for Expert Advice**

In certain situations, getting expert advice is crucial for your security and welfare. The following circumstances call for you to think about speaking with a fitness expert or healthcare provider:

1. Persistent Pain: See a healthcare professional if you have ongoing pain, discomfort, or an injury that doesn't go better with rest and self-care.

2. Lack of Progress: A fitness expert can offer advice and program modifications if you're not moving closer to your fitness objectives or if you've reached a standstill.

3. Pre-existing Health Conditions: Before beginning or altering your exercise regimen, speak with a healthcare physician or fitness professional if you have any pre-existing health conditions, are pregnant, or are experiencing any other medical issues.

4. New to Exercise: To make sure you're doing exercises with correct form and safety,

think about working with a fitness professional if you're new to exercising or trying a new, tough fitness program.

5. Complex Goals: A coach or certified trainer can offer the knowledge you require if your fitness objectives are intricate or specialized, such as getting ready for a particular sport or competition.

Long-term success in your fitness journey depends on making safety your top priority. Your fitness pursuits will be gratifying and injury-free if you maintain appropriate form, avoid common exercise-related injuries, and seek professional help when needed.

We'll provide you detailed workouts and routines in the upcoming chapters that emphasize safety and good form, giving you the confidence to work toward your fitness objectives and a lower chance of injury.

*Being fit is about strengthening your mind and body, not about breaking them.*

## Chapter 8: Fitness Psychology

Your journey towards fitness is greatly influenced by your mental attitude and thinking. This chapter delves into the psychology of fitness, emphasizing the development of a positive outlook, surmounting challenges, maintaining consistency, and the significance of monitoring advancements and acknowledging accomplishments.

**Developing an Upbeat Attitude**

Having an optimistic outlook will help you reach your fitness objectives. Here's how to develop an optimistic outlook:

1. Self-Compassion: Treat yourself with kindness. Recognize that obstacles and failures are normal parts of the path. Be kind to yourself and supportive of yourself as you would a friend.

2. Goal Visualization: Assume that your objectives have already been met. Your motivation will increase and your goals will seem more doable as a result.

3. Affirmations: To strengthen your confidence in your skills and abilities, use positive affirmations. Recite affirmations such as "I am strong" or "I am capable."

4. Keep Your Attention on the Process: Acknowledge minor victories along the way. Acknowledging even the smallest amount of progress will help you stay motivated.

5. Surround Yourself with Positive People: Assemble a group of people who encourage and uplift you on your fitness journey. Keep doubt and negativity at bay.

6. Mind-Body Connection: Recognize the link between your physical and mental health. A more resilient and energized physique might result from having a positive outlook.

**Overcoming Difficulties and Maintaining Uniformity**

Any fitness path will inevitably encounter obstacles, but they don't have to become impediments. Here's how to persevere in the face of difficulties:

1. Have Reasonable Expectations: Recognize that improvement takes time. Don't anticipate

outcomes right away. Maintain your commitment and patience throughout time.

2. Problem-Solve: When faced with challenges, take the time to examine the issue and brainstorm potential solutions.

3. Break It Down: Aiming high can be intimidating. To make them more attainable, divide them into smaller, more doable tasks.

4. Establish a Support Network by Talking to Friends, Family, and Workout Partners about Your Objectives. Accountability and motivation can be obtained via having a support network.

5. Accept Change: Keep an open mind and be willing to modify your plan as needed. Because life is full of changes, your exercise regimen should be flexible too.

6. Consistency Above Perfection: When it comes to your exercise regimen, consistency is more crucial than perfection. Don't worry if your plan somewhat changes.

## Monitoring Development and Honoring Success

Maintaining motivation and reaffirming your dedication to your fitness journey can be accomplished by routinely monitoring your progress and acknowledging your accomplishments. Read below ways to accomplish it:

1. Maintain a Workout Journal: List your exercises, accomplishments, and any difficulties you've encountered. It offers a visual illustration of your advancement.

2. Establish Checkpoints: Establish checkpoints or milestones for your fitness quest. Whether it's a substantial weight loss or a personal record, these are times to rejoice.

3. Reward Yourself: Give yourself a treat when you accomplish goals, such as a brand-new training attire or a soothing spa day.

4. Share Your Success: Don't be afraid to let your network of supporters know about your accomplishments. Sharing your achievements with others can foster a sense of belonging and motivation.

5. Reflect and Adjust: Evaluate your progress on a regular basis and make the required modifications to your objectives and goals. This maintains the movement and goal of your journey.

6. Pay Attention to Non-Scale Wins: Honor more than just the scale's reading. Acknowledge gains in general wellbeing, strength, endurance, and flexibility.

Fitness psychology is just as vital as the physical components. Your long-term success is influenced by a positive outlook, your capacity for problem-solving, and your habit of monitoring your development and acknowledging your accomplishments. We'll cover specific tactics, exercises, and routines in the upcoming chapters, all of which will help you stay mentally well and stay motivated as you pursue your fitness goals.

*Your thoughts are an effective instrument. If you train it properly, it will be your most valuable fitness tool.

## Chapter 9: Long-Term Health and Lifestyle

Your fitness journey is about long-term health and well-being, not just about reaching short-term objectives. This chapter will examine the close relationship between your lifestyle and fitness, as well as the effects of stress and sleep on fitness. It will also offer suggestions for developing long-lasting habits that will promote your long-term health.

### The Relationship Between Fitness and Lifestyle

Your long-term health and fitness journey are greatly impacted by the lifestyle decisions you make. Your fitness and lifestyle are linked in the following ways:

1. Nutrition: The food you eat gives your body the energy it needs to operate at its best. Energy, recuperation, and general health are all dependent on proper nutrition.

2. Activity Level: A key component of your fitness is your daily activity level, which includes both regular movement and scheduled workouts. Regular exercise

supports weight control, cardiovascular health, and general vitality.

3. Stress Management: Prolonged stress can impede the development of your fitness and cause health problems. The ability to effectively manage stress is crucial for maintaining good mental and physical health.

4. Sleep Quality: Restorative and rejuvenating sleep is essential for your body. It's critical for hormone balance, muscle restoration, and general health.

5. Habits and Routine: Your everyday routines, including time management, might have an impact on your fitness goals. Your everyday objectives for fitness might be aided by maintaining order and consistency.

## Stress, Sleep, and How They Affect Fitness

Getting enough sleep and managing your stress are essential for both your long-term health and fitness goals. How they affect your fitness is as follows:

1. Sleep: Getting enough sleep improves hormone regulation, cognitive performance, and muscle rehabilitation.

2. Stress: Prolonged stress raises the risk of injury, exhaustion, weight gain, and poor recovery. Use stress-reduction strategies, such as deep breathing, meditation, or relaxing hobbies.

3. Sleep and Exercise: Not getting enough sleep might make it harder to exercise and raise your chance of being hurt. Getting enough sleep increases the advantages of your exercise.

4. Exercise and Stress: Exercise is a good way to relieve stress. Frequent exercise can elevate mood, reduce stress, and enhance general wellbeing.

**Establishing Durable Routines for Extended Health**

The secret to long-term fitness and health is developing enduring habits. Here are some tips for creating and sustaining routines that promote your wellbeing:

1. Start little: Make little, sustainable adjustments at first that you can stick with. Steady, gradual changes yield greater results than abrupt, transient ones.

2. Consistency: Create a daily schedule that incorporates stress reduction methods, healthy eating, and exercise. Long-term success requires consistency.

3. Gradual Progress: As you develop habits, progressively up the degree of difficulty or intensity. This guarantees that you advance and push yourself further.

4. Accountability: Use a fitness app to monitor your progress or share your objectives with a friend. Having someone to answer to helps keep you on course.

5. Patience: Recognize that it takes time to form enduring habits. Recognize that obstacles are a part of the path and practice patience with yourself.

6. Periodic Assessments: Examine your routines and habits on a regular basis. Make the required modifications to make sure they stay in line with your health and fitness objectives.

7. Adjust to Change: Since life is dynamic, your routines should also adjust to new situations. Maintaining your routines' sustainability is ensured by their flexibility.

Your long-term health and fitness goals are directly impacted by the lifestyle decisions you make. You may support your fitness objectives and experience long-lasting well-being by making thoughtful decisions about your diet, exercise, sleep, and stress management. You may also do this by developing sustainable habits. We'll present certain tactics, workouts, and regimens that support a fit, healthy, and energetic lifestyle in the upcoming chapters.

*The decisions you make each day affect your long-term fitness and health. Select carefully.

## Chapter 10: Accepting Inner Strength and Moving Past the Physical

Although physical strength and attractiveness are frequently linked to fitness, it's also about developing inner strength and self-determination. This chapter will cover the value of self-assurance, how to become a better and happier version of yourself, and motivational tales from women who have changed their lives by exercise.

### Self-assurance and Self-determination

Your fitness journey is about more than simply getting a stronger body—it's about empowerment and self-assurance as well. This is the reason these factors are crucial:

1. Self-Confidence: Reaching your fitness objectives increases your self-assurance. The ability to create goals and put in the effort to achieve them carries over into other spheres of your life.

2. Empowerment: Being fit gives you the ability to take charge of your own health and wellbeing. It serves as a reminder that you are capable of changing your life for the better.

3. Mental Resilience: You gain the capacity to overcome hurdles and mental resilience by overcoming fitness-related problems.

4. Stress Reduction: Engaging in physical activity might help you feel less anxious and more mentally well.

5. favorable Body Image: Despite social norms, reaching fitness objectives frequently results in a more favorable body image.

6. Better Mental Health: Research shows that exercise improves mental health by lowering anxiety and depressive symptoms.

**The Path to a Happier, Healthier You**

The path to becoming a better and happier version of yourself is your fitness journey. This is how it benefits your general health:

1. Physical Health: Fitness increases general vitality, lowers the risk of chronic diseases, and improves cardiovascular health.

2. Mental Health: Physical activity improves mood and lowers stress, which encourages a more positive outlook.

3. Longevity: Living a healthy, active lifestyle is linked to a longer lifespan.

4. Energy and Productivity: Being fit gives you more energy, which makes it easier for you to do everyday tasks and be productive.

5. Quality of Life: Being fit improves your physical capabilities and opens up new things for you to engage in, which improves your quality of life.

6. Emotional Well-Being: Reaching fitness objectives makes you feel happy and accomplished.

You can attain physical and emotional well-being and design a life that is purposeful, colorful, and full of possibilities by embracing self-assurance, empowerment, and inner strength.

*You have the ability to shape your life in ways you never would have imagined thanks to your inner strength.

## Conclusion: Your Path to a Happier, Healthier You

We hope that this book has provided you with empowerment, direction, and inspiration as we come to the end of our fitness adventure. It's a transformative journey that will lead you to a healthier, happier version of yourself. It involves developing inner strength, self-confidence, and a sense of empowerment in addition to physical strength.

Achieving fitness involves taking care of your body, mind, and soul. It's about realizing your amazing potential, pushing past obstacles, and setting and attaining goals. You now understand the importance of a healthy diet, efficient exercise routines, and the principles of fitness, but you have also learned how closely lifestyle, mental health, and long-term health are related.

Keep in mind that inner strength, self-assurance, and empowerment are just as crucial as physical prowess. You have the chance to improve both inside and out through your fitness adventure. It's about acknowledging and appreciating not just the weight you can lift or the numbers on the scale, but also the self-assurance you've gained, the stress you've managed, and the joy you've discovered along the journey.

You have discussed the psychological components of fitness, the value of self-confidence, and the inspiring tales of women whose fitness journeys have changed their lives in the chapters that precede this conclusion. These tales serve as an example of the strength of willpower, resiliency, and inner fortitude.

Recall that progress, not perfection, is what matters as you proceed down your path to a healthier, happier version of yourself. Accept the trip, celebrate each milestone, and draw lessons from every misstep. Your path to fitness is a never-ending adventure that will continue to influence your life, health, and prospects.

# The Ultimate Women's Guide to Fitness: Fat-Burning Exercises and Workouts

We hope that this book will serve as a continuous companion for you on your journey, providing you with inspiration, knowledge, and practical strategies. Your dedication to your health and your exceptional inner strength are both strong indicators of your potential and resiliency.

Your fitness journey is just the beginning; you are capable of amazing things. As you proceed, celebrate the resilience you've developed, the self-assurance you've fostered, and the health you've preserved. You will become a better, happier version of yourself on this journey, which is yours.

*Accept your inner power and allow it to lead you to a life full of energy, health, and boundless opportunities.*

The Ultimate Women's Guide to Fitness: Fat-Burning Exercises and Workouts

Made in the USA
Monee, IL
16 March 2024